SOLVING
SCIENCE
MYSTERIES

Why Does Electricity Flow?

All About Electricity

Rob Moore

PowerKiDS press.

New York

Published in 2010 by The Rosen Publishing Group, Inc.
29 East 21st Street, New York, NY 10010

Produced and designed by Denise Ryan & Associates
Editor: Helen Moore and Edwina Hamilton
Designer: Anita Adams
Photographer: Lyz Turner-Clark
U.S. Editor: Joanne Randolph

Photo Credits: p. 4 top: © Photographer: Nikolai Sorokin | Agency: Dreamstime.com; p. 4 middle: © Photographer: Jaimie Duplass | Agency: Dreamstime.com; pp. 4 bottom, 7 and 16: DKimages; p. 5 bottom: © Photographer: Dan Bannister | Agency: Dreamstime.com; p. 5 bottom right: Yegor Korzh; p. 6: NOAA; p. 8 top © Photographer: David Pruter | Agency: Dreamstime.com; p. 8 middle left © Photographer: Aleksandar Jocic | Agency: Dreamstime.com; p. 8 middle right: © Photographer: Ilya Shmoylov | Agency: Dreamstime.com; p. 8 bottom: © Photographer: Michael Shake | Agency: Dreamstime.com; p. 10 top © Photographer: Anatoly Vartanov | Agency: Dreamstime.com; p. 10 second from top © Photographer: Grafikeray | Agency: Dreamstime.com; p. 10 bottom left: © Photographer: David Hyde | Agency: Dreamstime.com; p. 11: Aidan C. Siegel; pp. 12 top,16 top,19: Photolibrary; p. 12 middle: Thomas Ricks; p. 13 bottom: © Photographer: Nadejda Tebenkova | Agency: Dreamstime.com; p. 13 middle: © Photographer: Abbeychristine | Agency: Dreamstime.com; p. 14 middle left: © Photographer: Jon Kroninger | Agency: Dreamstime.com; p. 14 middle right: Salva Barbera; p. 14 bottom: Tony Clough; p. 15 top: Nathan Borror.

Library of Congress Cataloging-in-Publication Data

Moore, Rob, 1953–
 Why does electricity flow? : all about electricity / Rob Moore.
    p. cm. — (Solving science mysteries)
 Includes index.
 ISBN 978-1-61531-893-3 (lib. bdg.) — ISBN 978-1-61531-917-6 (pbk.) —
 ISBN 978-1-61531-918-3 (6-pack)
 1. Electricity—Miscellanea—Juvenile literature. I. Title.
 QC527.2.M66 2010
 537—dc22

                    2009034101

Manufactured in the United States of America

CPSIA Compliance Information: Batch #WW10PK: For Further Information contact Rosen Publishing, New York, New York at 1-800-237-9932

Contents

Questions About Electricity

Q: What is electricity?

A: Electricity is a form of energy produced by the movement of **electrons**. It can be used to heat up a toaster, **amplify** a guitar, or light a city. This is made possible by the production of electric currents, which are electric charges flowing along wires in a **circuit**.

on/off switch

light bulb

batteries

Q: Why does electricity flow?

A: Electricity flows when a source of energy works on moving an electric charge through a circuit. The energy can be movement, a chemical reaction, or even friction between two objects rubbing together. The electric charge flows through the circuit like water flows through pipes. Just as a water pump can act as the force for water in a pipe to flow, so can batteries or **generators** provide the force to make electricity flow.

Q: How is electricity made?

A: In Tasmania, Australia, over 90 percent of the electricity used is made from hydroelectricity, which is produced by the movement of water. The water is held in dams and released down pipes that lead to a turbine. The turbine turns a shaft, which rotates a series of magnets past copper coils and a generator to produce electricity. Power lines connected to the hydroelectric power station carry electricity to our homes, farms, and factories. The current that is carried inside the wires is alternating current, or AC, electricity. Electric power can also be generated by using nuclear fission, wind, oil, coal, or gas.

The Gordon Dam, on the Gordon River, Tasmania

Wind farms can be a source of electricity.

Questions About Static Electricity

Q: Does electricity occur naturally?

A: Electricity does occur naturally, in the form of lightning. This intense flash of heat and light is created by static electricity. The buildup of electric charge in a thunder cloud creates an opposite charge on the ground. Eventually a gigantic electric spark leaps between the two charges in a release of energy. The average stroke of lightning is about 6 miles (9.65 km) long. A lightning bolt would get to the Moon in about one second if it could travel that far. It is also hotter than the surface of the Sun.

Lightning is a spectacular example of static electricity.

Hair-Raising

If you run a balloon over your hair over and over again as fast as you can, watch what happens! The balloon brushes electrons onto your hair, giving each of your hairs the same type of charge. The hairs can't dump their extra charge so they repel each other, making them stand on end. This experiment works best on a dry day.

Q: What's the difference between static electricity and current electricity?

A: Static electricity occurs when electric charges build up but are not flowing. Most materials have no charge, but if a material gains or loses large numbers of electrons, it becomes charged with static electricity. Current electricity has a steady flow of electrons. Static electricity moves only when the charged material comes close enough to another material that has a large difference in free electrons. This table shows you the differences.

Static Electricity	Current Electricity
Is a buildup of electrons	Is the steady flow of electrons between objects or places. It travels along wires.
Stays in one place until it jumps to an object	Needs a conductor, a substance that allows electrons to move easily through it
Does not need a circuit	Needs a closed circuit to flow
Is the kind where you get a "shock" when you walk across a rug and then touch a door handle	The kind of electricity that powers the appliances and heat in your home (AC)
Lightning is a spectacular example of static electricity	The kind of electricity in a battery (direct current, or DC)

Questions About Batteries

Q: Can you store electricity?

A: Electricity can be stored in batteries but not in power plants. Electricity generated in power plants is used immediately.

Batteries provide portable power for such things as mobile phones, laptop computers, games, cameras, and flashlights. A chemical reaction produces their electricity. Batteries can be very small and placed in tiny medical or space research instruments but they can also be huge— big enough to power a car or earth-moving machines.

Electric cars run on batteries.

Q: Why do batteries die?

A: Batteries die when the chemicals inside them can no longer make electrons flow. The batteries contain chemicals that react together to separate positive and negative charges. This chemical reaction does not take place unless the positive and negative ends of a battery are connected to form a circuit. When the battery is connected and is producing electricity, the chemicals slowly change. Eventually they are not able to produce the chemical reaction needed and the electrons stop moving through the circuit. That is when the battery dies!

bulb

batteries in a flashlight

wire   *batteries*

Fruit Battery

Make your own battery using a **galvanized** nail, a copper coin, and a lemon. Insert the coin into a cut in one side of the lemon and push the nail into the other side. The nail and the coin must not touch. The lemon is now a single cell battery. The nail and the coin are the **electrodes** and the lemon juice is the **electrolyte**. Your battery won't run a motor or energize a light bulb but it will produce a dim glow from an LED.

Questions About Electricity at Home

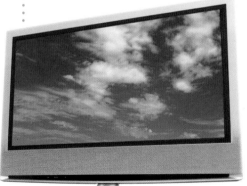

Q: Why do circuit breakers trip?

A: Circuit breakers act as a safety fuse for a house's electrical system. Circuit breakers usually trip, or cut off the power, because they have become overheated by too much power being drawn through them. For example, if the TV, air conditioner, clothes dryer, computer, and stereo are all on full power at the same time, a house circuit breaker is likely to overheat and trip. If the circuit breaker didn't trip, it is very likely one of the appliances would catch fire.

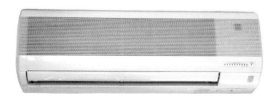

Q: Why does my iPod need an AC adapter?

A: An AC adapter must be used to change the powerful AC electricity from the wall point to the less powerful DC electricity that an iPod needs. The adapter also recharges the iPod's internal battery as chemical changes happen inside it to allow it to produce more electricity. Rechargeable batteries use different metals than those in single-use batteries.

It's a Fact

> First Electric Car

Robert Anderson of Scotland created the first official electric car, between 1932 and 1939. More a carriage than an actual car, it was a simple design that used nonrechargeable electric batteries for its power.

> Electric Guitar

The volume knob on an electric guitar works like a dimmer switch. When the knob is turned, two wires move nearer or farther apart along a piece of **graphite**. This varies the **voltage** that is available for the amplifier and loudspeaker.

> Night Light

Skyscrapers are lit by thousands of lights. The lights on each floor are part of a different branch of a large parallel circuit. When security guards patrol a building at night, they can turn on one branch of the circuit at a time. This makes the lights glow on just one floor, saving electricity.

> Show Off

Electricity was first used in homes in the late 1800s. At that time electricity was so expensive that people only put lights in their most important rooms. Some people, who could only afford one lightbulb, decided to put it in the hall. They left the light on all day—even when they were out—to show it off to passersby.

> Supply and Demand

Electricity generated by power stations is fed into a national grid of interconnecting power lines. These take the energy to wherever it is needed. When you switch on a light, you have no way of knowing which power station the electricity came from.

Overhead transmission lines distribute electrical energy.

Can You Believe It?

Lightning Strike

There are about 100 lightning strikes on the planet every second, but the chances of actually being struck by lightning are around 1 in 3 million. However, you have more chance of being struck by lightning than winning the lottery, which is about 1 in 14 million!

Stand Back!

The scientist who discovered the electron, J. J. Thomson, was so clumsy that his students wouldn't let him go near his own equipment!

Pinball Buzz

The steel ball in a pinball machine bridges the gap between the target and the base of the machine. This completes a circuit that makes lights glow and buzzers buzz. The circuit switches off in an instant as the ball moves around.

Watch Out!

If you were to scuff your feet along the ground for long enough without touching anything, it would be possible to generate enough static electricity to blow off your fingers.

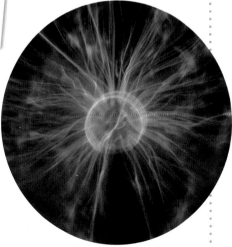

Who found Out?

Electric force: Alessandro Volta

Count Alessandro Volta (1745–1827) was an Italian physicist who invented the electric battery in 1800. First named the Voltaic pile, it was the forerunner of the electric battery and produced a steady, if relatively weak, electric current. Volta's battery was made of zinc, silver, and salt water. It was the model that Faraday used in his experiments. In 1810, Napoleon recognized Volta's work by making him a count. Count Volta was honored by having the unit for electric force, the volt, named after him.

Electric Dynamo: Michael Faraday

Michael Faraday (1791–1867) was an English chemist and physicist who contributed a great deal to our understanding of electricity. Regarded as a natural philosopher, someone who studied nature and the physical universe before the advent of modern science, Faraday performed many of the first known experiments with electricity.

His first battery was made of copper coins, sheets of zinc, and salt water. He also built the first electric motor and the electric **dynamo**, which was the forerunner of modern power generators. The measure of electric charge, the Farad, is named after Michael Faraday.

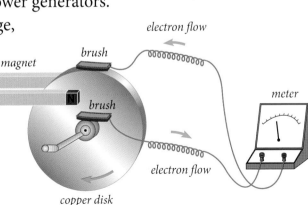

This is an illustration of Faraday's disk dynamo, the world's first electrical generator.

magnet

brush

brush

electron flow

electron flow

meter

copper disk

Light Up Your Life:
Thomas Edison

Thomas Edison (1847–1931) was an American inventor and businessman who has been credited with inventing many of the devices that we use in our daily lives. Edison has over one thousand **patents** credited to him in the United States, as well as many in the United Kingdom, France, and Germany. He is renowned for making the first lightbulb, but he shared the honor (and profit) of its invention with Joseph Swan. Edison also developed the first system for supplying electricity to buildings over a wide area.

Alternating Current: Nikola Tesla

Nikola Tesla (1856–1943) was born in Serbia and later became an American citizen. He was a world-famous inventor, physicist, and engineer. He performed much of the early research on electricity, which resulted in the AC system being adopted as a standard in most countries throughout the world. His battle with Edison to have AC electricity adopted rather than DC made him famous during his lifetime. However, in later life his eccentric personality and extreme claims about the possibilities of science saw him thought of as a "mad scientist." Tesla died poor and forgotten but in recent times has been given credit for his genius.

It's Quiz Time!

The pages where you can find the answers are shown in the red circles, except where otherwise noted.

Unscramble these famous scientists' names

1. Steal an kilo   (19)

2. Sorta love sandal   (16)

3. Day far achime la   (17)

4. Mad shoe is not   (18)

Find the 12 words hidden in this electricity grid

Answers on bottom of page 21.

E	W	L	B	L	D	V	R	X	S	R	Y	K	M	W
L	N	H	I	J	W	E	P	A	T	T	O	R	J	H
C	U	I	W	G	P	N	L	W	I	B	D	N	M	O
O	W	Y	B	P	H	T	R	C	R	S	G	N	G	V
N	P	S	O	R	W	T	I	Y	R	E	T	T	A	B
D	I	C	Z	A	U	R	B	E	Y	V	E	S	O	U
U	G	Y	M	T	T	K	U	F	T	J	A	C	C
C	K	E	V	C	N	U	V	J	L	U	Q	L	Z	I
T	R	U	E	Q	Z	I	N	C	D	B	L	E	J	T
O	H	L	S	R	Y	N	L	W	K	C	D	A	Y	A
R	E	B	X	E	L	I	G	H	T	N	I	N	G	T
B	J	F	T	W	I	I	K	K	L	G	C	I	E	S
H	Y	D	R	O	E	L	E	C	T	R	I	C	F	C
I	U	G	Q	P	J	V	F	L	V	R	M	R	D	V

Battery
Conductor
Copper
Electricity
Hydroelectric
Lightbulb
Lightning
Saltwater
Static
Turbine
Power
Zinc

True or false?

1. You have a better chance of winning the lottery than being struck by lightning. (14)

2. A small battery can be made using a lemon, a copper coin, and a zinc nail. (9)

3. The average stroke of lightning is about 6 miles (9.65 km) long. (6)

4. Electricity was first used in homes in the late 1900s. (13)

Scientists' ages

Of the four scientists in "Who Found Out?":

1. Who lived to the oldest age? (19)

2. Who died at the youngest age? (17)

3. Who was born earliest? (16)

4. Who was born most recently? (19)

Try It Out!

Turn to page 7 and read the sidebar about how static electricity works again. We are going to put those ideas into action.

What You'll Need: a blown-up balloon and a notebook

What to Do:

1 Rub the balloon on your hair several times as fast as you can. Now hold the balloon against the wall and let go. Does it stay on the wall? Repeat this step, but try to stick the balloon to different objects, such as a window. Write down what happens.

2 Now go into your bathroom, close the door, and turn on the shower for a few minutes. Rub the balloon on your hair again and try to stick it to the wall. Did it work? Static electricity forms more easily where it is cool and dry.

Glossary

alternating current (OL-ter-nayt-ing KUR-ent) Electricity that flows back and forth very fast through a wire.

amplify (AM-pluh-fy) To make louder.

circuit (SER-ket) An electrical network having at least one closed path for the flow of current.

conductor (kun-DUK-ter) A substance through which electrical charges can easily flow, such as wool, salt, water, and metals.

direct current (dih-REKT KUR-ent) Electricity where the electrons flow in one direction, as in a battery.

dynamo (DY-nuh-moh) A generator, especially one for producing direct current.

electrodes (ih-LEK-trohdz) Conductors by which electrons enter, leave, or are controlled within an electric device.

electrolyte (ih-LEK-truh-lyt) A substance that conducts electricity.

electrons (ih-LEK-tronz) The negatively charged particles that form the basis of electricity.

galvanized (GAL-vuh-nyzd) Coated with molten zinc.

generator (JEH-neh-ray-tur) A device that converts one form of energy to another.

graphite (GRA-fyt) A soft, greasy-feeling form of carbon.

nuclear fission (NOO-klee-ur FIH-shun) The splitting apart of atoms to release energy.

patents (PA-tents) The official rights given to an inventor to make or sell inventions for a certain time without them being copied.

turbine (TER-byn) A motor in which shafts are turned by the action of water, steam, coal, wind, or gas.

voltage (VOHL-tij) The differences in electric current measured by volts.

Index

Web Sites

Due to the changing nature of Internet links, PowerKids Press has developed an online list of Web sites related to the subject of this book. This site is updated regularly. Please use this link to access the list: *www.powerkidslinks.com/SSM/flow/*